Worth

Publication of this book has been supported

by a generous grant from the Greenwall Fund of

The Academy of American Poets

KUHL HOUSE POETS

Edited by Jorie Graham and Mark Levine

Worth

POEMS BY ROBYN SCHIFF

UNIVERSITY OF IOWA PRESS  IOWA CITY

University of Iowa Press, Iowa City 52242
Printed in the United States of America

Design by Richard Hendel

www.uiowapress.org

The publication of this book was generously supported
by the University of Iowa Foundation.

Printed on acid-free paper

Library of Congress Cataloging-in-Publication Data
Schiff, Robyn.
    Worth: poems / by Robyn Schiff.
        p.   cm.–(Kuhl House poets)
     ISBN 0-87745-820-0 (pbk.)
     I. Title.   II. Series.
    PS3619.C365 W67   2002
    811'.6–dc21   2002018059

FOR NICK

Contents

Acknowledgments

Sincere thanks to the editors of the following journals, where some of these poems first appeared: *Black Warrior Review, Explosive, Fence, Iowa Journal of Cultural Studies, Verse, Volt*, and *3rd Bed*.

Thank you, Mark Levine, the Iowa Writers' Workshop, and the University of Iowa Press. "Gypsy Rose" is for Michael Bray. "Industrial Diamonds" is for Lana Moussa; many thanks to her.

With gratitude to my mother and my father.

House of Worth

To trim the hat made to match the fifth white dress worn
this year, a feather of the mourning dove left this morning on the windowsill.

Dresses meant to be worn
once and once only and then worn
by servants lifting
the hem to hurry down the hall. Face worn,
dress quite new.

So many of Marie Antoinette's dresses were worn
to Masquerade last night, the hem of one dress
met the next dress
in waltz-time and the mind, time-worn
flung its doors
between compartments like the locomotive doors

in which Margaret Lockwood in *The Lady Vanishes* goes door
to door to find the truth. The tweed dress worn
to travel; pillbox hat, no veil, two pins; nothing. Margaret Lockwood watches one door
when the train stops and Michael Redgrave, who loves her already, watches the other door.

Remembering the Vanished Lady writing her name in the window-
fog is not a clue. She may have written it herself, the conductor said, and did
indeed suffer a blow to the head outside her hotel door.

The dress was so big,
one's hand is useless to take glass from table;
the skirt approaches while the hand is yet distanced.

At home, the dresses
are wider than doors

and carried one by one into the room she'll wear them, white dresses
are slipped over white dresses—
whole seasons worn
in the stead of one all dressed up
because she who has nowhere to go is most free. Dressed
to listen for the returning hunt; dressed
to see three deer stop by the apple tree near the closest window,
and didn't they come quietly? The window
was open. The wind sought the innermost layer and lifted
the dresses apart.

                                Lifting
                                the lid off the box, the Princess of Corinth
                                saw the gold dress and lifted
                                it out. She lifted
                                the dress in the mirror. She shut the door
                                and lifted
                                her old dress off. The children lifted
                                their hands to their eyes. Was there warning?
                                The room was hot. Was there warning?
                                The windows
                                were locked, so when I went to the window
                                there was nothing to do but bang on the window.

In 1878 hemlines lifted.
The window
would not. The window
sash could be tied to the leg of the dressing-
table and lowered down if the window
would open. The table would drag toward the window
when we climb down the ladder. There are doors

that never open with doors
behind them. On the previous night, she looked from the carriage window
as she passed the Princess's parlor window.
She saw him inside when the curtain lifted.

"What an admirable artist who makes us weep thus, two evenings in succession,
with the same words gives me the sensation that she is a different woman the
second day from the first.

When the dying Marguerite lets the mirror fall, it breaks. The first evening leaning
on the table, without gathering up the pieces, she looked at it with terror and
spoke to it from faraway, leaving this world.

This evening, kneeling down slowly, she goes right up to it, her outstretched hand
trembling, she collects the pieces."

Maison Cartier

1925 Exhibition of Arts of Decoration, Delayed by war, ten years.

Facing out: diamond/onyx machine-age stripes. Facing in: a clock as constant
as the heart and as well hidden. In lipstick-cases, powder-cases, cigarette-cases,
    a pair
of them: Paris-time/New York; Lisbon/New Port News; *You Set The Clock, We Set*
    The Gems. Constant
reminder: *I count the hours until . . .* ; For the constantly
delayed: a gift of beauty and practicality: *Where*
Are You? Form in constant
sync with function swinging from the very string of pearls. Constant
time-check startles?: an onyx bracelet linked by diamonds. Parting
from a quiet onyx, two roads leave darkness. Parts
refract. There is no constant.
Is it depression
hoarding everything in swimming black? Pressing

the pulse, onyx keeps. Depression
is the memory of everything constantly
darkening, bead pressing
bead pressing
bead. Abacus upon which all counts equally, the complex pared,
Need, Crux, Clasp. Light pressed
into onyx stays pressed —
memory up so close to glass it feels what it has been kept from from where
it has been kept. Where desire paces, memory wears
a path between window, door, and bed. It presses
you to check the locks. Asks Is it safe now, even to part
the curtains *this much* where the view is best? Part

of you wants to sleep all day. Part
wants to run down the front steps.
Cartier's platinum re-setting of a Queen's pear-shaped diamonds. Diamonds cut in
the eighteenth century reset so gracefully they seem to
just be there naturally of the will of diamond. The
platinum setting is stronger than gold and rarer; rarely
used until 1905 when Cartier showed diamond against it:
here tiny triangular cuts like carets indicate where part
was added. Platinum occurs in alluvial sands, but scant evidence exists of use by
ancients; near modern LaTolita, Esmeraldas, Ecuador,
pre-Columbians . . . "On Subtlty," 1557 . . . When Louis
XV sent Don Antonio de Ulloa to measure the meridian,
1748, he was taken prisoner of England. "We are not at
War with the arts and sciences," they told him, published
his papers. "I take the freedom to include to you an
account of a semi-metal called *Platina di Pinto.*" Constant
experiments follow. When Chabaneau removed gold,
mercury, lead, copper, iron, etc from the would-be
platinum, he was mistaken. He was left six undiscovered
metals instead of one: parts
so integrated he could not part
them. 1783, compressed pure platinum: white hot, hammered until it cohered. But
the pear-
shaped pair
of earrings was not made with it. Part
of everything is sad. She wore
them until the war.

Resetting them for exposition, Cartier was aware
he had acquired a vital part
of History. When taken Prisoner of Revolution in '91 Marie Antoinette was wearing
them. "Wear
them for me" Louis XVI said, perceiving these the perfect gift to offer his depressed
Queen. They require stature of the wearer:
a neck long enough to keep the pear-drop off the shoulder. But it wears
a girl down: 20.34 carats on the left, 14.25 on the right, one is aware of the constant
weight of wealth; and the earrings were a burden at certain times to privacy. Constantly
bothered by ears lately ringing, the Queen assumed "somewhere
someone in the Provinces must be talking about my jewelry." She served stewed pears
that first night she wore them. For days the Royal Chef halved pears

by the bushel so the Court-entire was pear-
enticed and no one thought of apples. It is touching to think of it: the Queen wearing
her own pair
of diamond pears
above their botanical counterpart
presented in the famous silver stewed-pear
bowls whose concavity matched the slightness of the very skin of pears.
All this, for the economy: the subtle depression
of the dinner plates called for one subtly depressed
employee of the state stationed at each guest's pear
plate ladling creme and chocolate sauce constantly.
And this for years, for History states, she wore the earrings "constantly."

Tiffany & Co.

How close the fire is to the fire screen.
Fire screen water birds below moons at intervals.
Patient glass-gloved hands offering water to them.

The dissolving moon-marsh grows tulips
more fragile than tulips.

Shifting behind the fire screen fire inhabits the girl,
the brook, the birds who come alive
glassy and glazed. Nothing moving, just flickering—

a projector stopped still on one frame which must be endured.
The Queen in *Rosita*, for instance, aligning her compact mirror away from her face
sees the King her husband holding Rosita, played by Mary Pickford,

on which the Queen's beauty is based.
Imagine the Queen in *Rosita* aligning her compact mirror
to see the room behind her forever. Glassy and glazed,

how fiery the face is behind her. In privileged lighting,
Mary Pickford's lighting the King's face as she leans forward.
How close beauty can come to its target;

the actress playing the queen was chosen
to show off the superior stare of Mary Pickford.
Irritation and desire forever in gray scale,

she regards the movie house audience drawn
to Mary Pickford spliced into her compact mirror.
Invisible Queen, I remember you,

Mary Pickford more fragile
than Mary Pickford.

In *Stella Maris*, Mary Pickford
as Unity Blake (left), and Stella Maris (right).

As Unity Blake and Stella Maris
there was Mary Pickford, a doorframe,
then Mary Pickford.
Speaking kindly to Mary Pickford,

there was Mary Pickford
(for she was kind as Stella Maris).
Speaking kindly back to Mary Pickford,
shy as Unity Blake, Mary Pickford said little.

For she was kind as Stella Maris,
Mary Pickford forgave the awkwardness
of Mary Pickford, shy as Unity Blake.
There is a flash of white light between them.

Mary Pickford, forgive the awkwardness
of the reel. Flashing white light,
your body's strobe,

furious. The reel, flashing
as if fire in the distance
was throwing a strobe. How close the fire is!

1912, car chase, *A Beast at Bay*, you with escaped convict
on the right bank of a brook, locomotive on the left,
death-chase reflected

in the intermingled
mirror of the brook

in which your pursuer
meets your savior

in one negotiation
with the speed of film.

There are times in a horse's gait when all four feet are off the ground.

'It is exciting, but one cannot tear oneself away.'

By alternating scenes rapidly, flash after flash:
cottage
field
mountaintop
sea

field
drawing-room
sea
steeplechase
we have a conversation between places rather than persons.

'There are two sides of it,' continued Karenin, 'that of the performers and that of the
spectators.'

In the motion picture gallery . . . these spectators are not a unit.

Anna said nothing, but without putting down her glasses looked steadily at one point . . .
'I am a bad
woman.
There was first laid before us . . .
the marvelous apparatus . . .
Each seizes upon the image
as it appears before it in an instant.'

Each marvelous apparatus,
has a string attached to it.

As it appears before it in an instant,
the trotting horse triggers the apparatus
by dislodging the string attached to it.

The horse behaved improperly today.
It threw its rider. The film was wasted.
There was despair I was unable to conceal.

'My race is a harder one,' replied Karenin, respectfully.

'You behaved improperly today.'
'How did I behave improperly?'
'The despair you were unable to conceal
when one of the riders fell.'

'*How* did I behave improperly?
There are times in a horse's gait when all four feet are off the ground.
When one of the riders fell,
I could not look away.'

Chanel N°5

Waterfall gown with water-
fowl sleekness embroidered so as to rise
with the speed of light while
not in motion; slit placed
to stride from standstill to escape
as a leopard, monkey, or fox might hear an en-
emy in the dark brush

before she sees it (the coat
is lined) and try deception. These Exiled
Russian Princesses em-
broidering with Pari-
sian seamstresses learned the over-
under stitch in which the end is drawn beneath the
fabric. In photos, fire

in the fireplace a blur on
a log—the shutter was slow—workers pose
as fire beyond betrays
the presentation. If
The Grand Duke Dimitri had moved
suddenly to kiss Chanel's mouth this also would
be recorded as a

blur. Yes, he who pushed Rasput-
in from the bridge pressed and held his mouth to
hers until light sufficed
to keep the exiled Duke
loving her. Action mustn't take
place on the surface but in illusive spaces.
Hesitant Princes of

no domain line up on a
gold chain upon the black drop of her dress
in the dark room. Her neck-
lace is all that shows up.
Patterns of points into inde-
pendent linear shapes transformed by Perspective
on which the cold light of

her jewelry surfaces
like the searchlights of a search-boat, body
in the river decom-
posing, murderer, free.
"At my age, when a man wants you
you don't ask to see his passport," she answered re-
porters about fucking

the Nazi called "The Sparrow"
(his language) in 1940 when in-
vited back to Paris
to fuck him at the Ritz.
Emptiness is innocent? Not
so as Ruth Greenglass described a hollow in the
stereo-console in the

sitting room of her in-laws
in which a lamp was installed. For use in
microfilming, a bulb
affixed on the secret
documentation of the bomb
delicately renders that which is put before
it; reiterating,

smaller, in the Rosenbergs'
console, the atom bomb assembling
and assembling in
silent darkness. Visit-
ors want to hear a record, the
Rosenbergs say the stereo is broken. We've
been waiting on repair-

men almost since we bought it.
There's no workmanship. Mrs. Rosenberg
who unscrewed the transmitt-
er herself says something
must be missing under the lid,
I lifted it and it looked lost.

The Rosenberg testimon-
y admits an ordinary living-
room, a stereo they
paid $21
for. Inside, nothing unusu-
al. A maid they paid too much dusted it every
second Friday morning.

House of Dior

Now we are on the chapter of pleats.
The impatience to fold, the joys of having folded,
the pleasures of folding them again.
Fabric enough in the sleeve to drape the dress,
in the skirt to drape a chest of drawers,
in the dress to drape the view of trees blacked-out
along the walk from here to the next
house. Walking in the dark inside the house
this is the black we black the windows with.
I have hung the last square of cloth.
Good-bye porch. Good-bye midnight postman
with your sack of envelopes. My love sings
to himself. Each pleat steps into the seam
with a pin in its mouth. Crease upon crease,
a fan on which an embroidered rowboat sits
at the far edge of a lake. The lake is deep enough.

House of Versace

When the
suspect
touched the
corpse and
the corpse
bled a-
new, it
was proof
in New
England.
Surely
there would
be a
sign when
Robins
saw the
body.
Rosi-
na touched
a small
amount
of Wat-
er of
the Dawn
to each
of the
offic-
er's hand-
kerchiefs.

It was
left how
it was

left when
Helen
met the
inspect-
or (Ros-
ina
asked could
she straight-
en Hel-
en's night
dress be-
fore the
press came.)
(No, she
may not.).

When an-
ything
falls we
call it
Helen
falling
even
if it
was one
of us
who dropped
the glass.
Helen,
elsewhere,
by now
would be
too lost

to ev-
en haunt
us, Ros-
ina
said, pour-
ing tea
in a
report-
er's tea-
cup. "There,"
she said,
"hot tea."

Helen
was drawn
all wrong.
I did
not see
the bod-
y, but
one girl
saw it.
Helen
was not
waiting
with one
shoulder
showing
for who
is her
lover
to lie
down be-

side her,
Is it
morning,
asking
is it
morning
it is
morning
now is-
n't it.

There must
be clues
we live
with we
don't take
as clues.

We were
in the
parlor—
Robins,
two stran-
gers, Hel-
en, anoth-
er girl.
After
the one
calling
himself
Joseph
paid me

he went
home a-
round one-
thirty
(It says
in my
journal
1:30.).
And I
had a
bath but
I slept
some in
the bath
when you
want me
to know
if I
heard Rob-
ins, I
just fell
asleep
as soon
as I
touched the
water.

"Witness
said he
don't know
the Cloak
but has

seen the
suspect
wear a
Cloth Cloak
simi-
lar to
the one
shown him.
—As near
like it
as is
one Cloth
Cloak a-
nother."

When, to
keep him,
after
his vic-
tory
in the
winding
halls, she
gave in-
to his
hand the
thread you
see there
where the
Cloak had
caught. On-
ly a
woman

could know
it— it
was Hel-
en's hand
that sewed
it, Thread
oft caught
up ag-
ain and
passed through
the hands
led on
by it.

(Witness
said he
don't know
the Cloak
but has
seen the
suspect
wear a
Cloth Cloak
simi-
lar to
the one
shown him.)

The Cloth
Cloak has
string tied
inside
the lin-

ing the
same as
string tied
around
the hand-
le of
the hatch-
et found
inside
the court-
yard fence.
Some twen-
ty-five
hundred
hatchets
like this
were sold
since eight-
een thir-
ty four,
the own-
er of
the firm
that stamped
the hatch-
et said.
The port-
er in
Hoxie's
firm where
Robins
clerks who
uses

such a
hatchet
open-
ing box-
es missed
one Mon-
day morn-
ing. "From
the dark-
est marks
upon
it, and
from its
being
blunted"
Hoxie's
porter
knew the
hatchet.

When Rob-
ins came
inside
the house
I re-
member
Helen
grasping
Robins'
hands at
once and
saying
Robins'

hands were
freezing.
It was
a freez-
ing night
mine were
freezing.
Thinking
how the
hatchet
must have
swung tied
inside
that Cloak,
it is-
n't what
I like
to think
about
but I
think the
hatchet
must have,
with the
Cloak closed
around
it, been
swinging.

(Just the
thinnest
thread that
held it)

Holding,
I
am hold-
ing, I
am lett-
ing you

go, (the
string that
held the
hatchet)

Helen
led a-
stray

me
and
ering

loose

where is
the op-
ening?

the arc
of stor-
y hold-
ing and
holding
is lett-
ing you
fall

Where is
the op-
ening?

The last
witness
who owns
the to-
bacco
shop spoke
with Rob-
ins as
Robins
sat on
a wood-
en barr-
el smok-
ing tob-
acco
"It was
the hour
concern-
ing us.
I am
not a
prosti-
tute my
[word]
is mine"

Open-
ing and
open-
ing on

(I re-
membered
the world
when he
entered
with a
wet um-
brella)

the op-
ening

(and I
was ash-
amed.).

Devil Finch

Red eyes on a red-feathered head seem not to be watching
or seem to be watching and are not,
self-camouflaged, unreliably witnessing the
war cries of the Hoop-hoop rippling visibly up the body
adrenaline firing cutthroat against the rope
of the larynx unbalanced in fits, a scream
that calls the firefly off the firefly, you do not hear it, devil finch,
fit to survive obliviously
appetiteless, instinct has left you listless
on an electric wire in which
500,000 megahertz course toward
the doorknob, glibly static.

Lack says you want this.
Hearing of a red without flux, suspiciously red red at which light turns and
goes back to its source   A red field on a map of which the legend
says: red   Draw me after you, let us make haste. Red has brought me into its
chamber   My mind goes red at the thought of you, love   You woke out
of dream breathless and flushed, as if pursued for hours   The quill of the
red devil finch: 42% red, 8% red, 50% red   Hearing of it she wanted it
and as she was Queen, sent a fleet
(Dear Garden Sirs,
          Does it not reflect poorly upon the Gardener that the Garden is without?

Dear Tapestry-Master,
          Where does the devil finch nest in your design?

Dearly Appointed Chef,
          I am dissatisfied.)
                              In rooms dark enough to rouse the listening-self to its
feet, the devil finch, just out of ear-reach, can be heard by those who hearing all
things in the heaven hear that nothing has been said there   Nor do leaves rustle

when nothing moves them   Nor has the devil finch disturbed anyone
excepting how a phone not ringing reveals loneliness is disturbing
          A decoy has too much
          that was formed by hands
          desiring to hold one

See the disinterest with which devil finch approaches devil finch
or how the hired captor abandons quest when the devil finch perches restfully on
his issued gun;

"I never really wanted one," he wrote his lover
"Nor am I coming home."

There were two men
dead in the morning.
It had nothing to do
with the devil finch
watching

nor do I believe from what I saw in Patagonia
that when an animal is killed
elsewhere
in the jungle
the devil finch
soon gains
intelligence
of it.

Good-Bye Finch

When that which closes
hopes. Better to
measure. Leaner
weaves the raven
nearer the center, our
single reminder which the black bird makes
"find me, I am here" music,
crying out
"this food is not filling." Find me
time, pleasure, ocean, ever,
or pure abstraction
as if the lightness

Forget that which is
rare? ounce? blessed?
Do you know the word for
what you do not
want. Transactions take place
Always a disruption
Transactions take the place of you

Vampire Finch

Roosting in a crater with one
red foot on either side of her stony egg,
the red-footed booby endures the finch
feeding on her tail in which the
finch has inserted its intravenous
bill to drink the blood. The red-footed booby
knows what happens if she steps

from duty to shoo the finch. The
finch's bill the ages perfect with use will
pierce the egg with one thrust and leave the egg,
should someone come along, fit to
paint an easter meditation upon
that can never spoil. A lacquer developed
by the Japanese who had

no easter, also uses egg
shell and no egg. Cracked beyond recognition,
the fragments are inlaid so as to seem one
continuous flat surface of
a tabletop on which one writing home
never knows one leans one's elbows on that which
stood balanced alone on its

smallest point, vernal equinox
momentarily drawing the whole egg up;
likewise, darkly drawing, the vampire finch
draws on the red-footed booby's
tail-blood; it attaches itself in the
air like Spanish moss, is already feeding
when it puts its feet down on

the feathered back of its warm source.
Pictured feeding itself, iconography
perfect for an island flag or stone-cut
sculpture through which water runs off
the roof of a church through the open beak
of one bird into the beak of the vampire
into the courtyard spouting

black rain filthy from the carved gut
of both ugly birds, finch tense with appetite,
victim-bird rigid with patience and blood
loss, the weakening stance of its
roost captured in Peter's Basilica
where Jesus firmly droops across Mary. The
inevitability

of the finch's thirst darts into
the arrowy point of the beak that stands in
nature for Dracula's two pointed teeth
inscribing a sleepy neck with
marks a prisoner makes to count two more
days with the tine of a fork. When he doesn't
hunt his own, slaves bag village

children and leave them struggling on
the Count's floor, beds empty when parents check them
in the morning. How do they get in? There was
no disturbance but a storm in
the distance rocking a cargo ship in
and out of the beam of the lighthouse. The Count
was in the hold of that ship

raising the coffin lid off the
coffin he traveled in. On land in a train
racing the ship, Mina raises her arms
in a trance in which she gestures
emptily as the Count eats through
the unsuspecting watchmen of the ship's crew,
the smell of shit in the air

makes Mina too sick to eat her
own meal her companions offer. On the ship,
flies breed in the wet muck. More beautiful
than the flower petal in the
prismatic bubble the male fly brings the
female, the empty bubble he sometimes brings
instead. Revolving in the

glassy glare like a globe Vermeer
would dangle, it would make you sick to see things
as fast as they happen like locking your
gaze on a passing train you have
to look away. Loeb did when Leopold
practiced passing ransom from the 3 o'clock.
He looked away from train to

cigar box to marsh grass searching
for the empty box which would contain ransom
if this wasn't practice. Leopold knew
a good place to hide the body
from his days of bird-watching where the train
cut through the still marsh and "From the air vents we
could see civilians laughing."

Vest-Pocket Finch

oh little-willed feathers rearranged
upon a decorated hat as the tail of a taller bird,
isn't this the dime that was your throne?
oh surveillance of the soul
that watches the soul yearn,

isn't that you,
hors d'oeuvre? Doll house
doll house furniture stool
on which the doll's
doll steps
to reach the clock
in the imagination's
second parlor? Isn't
this the room
she lost one shoe?
Isn't this the brooch
you dropped on the second Stepping-Stone
ribbon of disappearing Islands
off your coast?

Forget
this note
in which
the brooch
was wrapped.

St. Lucia Finch

Knowing it is the plumage that burns
five shades of fire ranging from incite to ever-
lasting that is prized by the English,
when the feather merchant replaced
the innards with dry leaves he also snipped the worthless
legs on which the bird withstood

her nestlings' cries when the feed was gone
and the box came down. When the Court Painter of New
Species unloaded it from a box
of birds, each facing the tail of
another in the manner of shipped glasses, years of
wayfaring interrupted

his memory of seeing how the
St. Lucia finch standing on a pillar built to
moor boats reminded him of one of
twin torches and he sketched it here
legless, flying-intent with no footstep, those sandy
quotations beside the trap

that transcribe the route the robin takes
or the deposed King who speechlessly proceeding
up rue Saint-Honoré, confessor
astride, kept pace with the marching
drummers, each behind another except a marshal
whose stride times a soldier in

his mind's eye splicing the rope that keeps
the guillotine blade aloft until the moment
of departure. When the head of state
is lost, the body politic
stands for itself in the bright road, a torch in daylight
burning for itself. Drawn

in flight in three-quarter aspect from
beside and below, the St. Lucia finch eyes perch
after perch of sill from which to curse
the rooms inside if only it
could stand over the mood from the ledge with its brief soul
selling the course of events

within, instantiating in stance
the mind and body both, I think, and for the soul,
a stolen button in the lining
of its nest attaching nothing
to nothing. Pictured endlessly unable to land
on the nursery sill with-

out a pair of legs echoing in
their duplicity the partnership in which the
shadow and the self place broken bits
in the shallow bottom of a
broken glass, the depicted St. Lucia finch in turn
maps a bird's-eye view wanton

with hazards of misstep where every
cornice head on which a bird by right should land is
chiseled so as to appear hanging
severed in the instant between
the blade and death, during which, with prior arrangements,
you can communicate with

a witness by fluttering your eyes
in a manner agreed between you to mean Yes,
there is pause in what is conceived
as the instantaneousness
of death to continue with a friend on the subject
of mourning for yourself. "In

all honesty," the friend noted, "I
could not decipher our code to say there was a
sentence spoken certainly with the
eyes, or if the muscles, released
from domination, fluttered on their own as if flirt-
ing with our God for pardon."

Woodpecker Finch

That bird named for the bird twice-size itself
has a twig in its mouth or would not be called
the woodpecker finch, extending its reach the length of a twig,
it probes the bark for ants

with the twig in its mouth it would not be called
the woodpecker finch without.
It probes the bark for ants
in darkness where the dead were brought—

woodpecker finch, without,
ruts of ants, within, collapsed
in darkness where the dead were brought
down on the living like salt

salting salt. Being stealthy,
being invisible,
poking with a puppet like a hyphen into
the colony while the finch is yet in the transept of the church,

machine-tragedy in which God cranked from rafters
is not the Japanese black-cloaked puppeteer walking among the living
story of a wife whose devotion to her husband is such she throws herself
from a cliff. The woodpecker finch

sticks the stick-faced stick into the sappy bark,
naked, jerking from the beak of the finch,
picking at the sand with its one foot,
what god is this without a mask

coming or going
like a snake
that won't bend?

Goddess of Mercy
mercifully intervened
and saved the wife.

A bobby pin in an electric socket
plugged into the current
without being dropped
in front of the outlet.

Plugged into the current,
Bridge of Emergencies
from the outlet
to the outer

colony? No. The finch's extended beak
jutting from its given beak,
temporary, light enough to lift in flight,
resolved: *look look* (the theater is dark)

look look (finch taps prop).
A play using multiple sets
provides contrast when a god
causes one place to vanish

mid-act. Flying machines,
trapdoors, hidden stairs,
plot twists, tricks of light,
gloved hands,

promptbooks.
There is music.
There is little conversation.
Wife escapes singing

through the stage door
where the stagehand leans between acts.
Who will fill the wineglass for the love scene?
Who will fall in love?

The final configuration of the B-2 Stealth Bomber
"flies by wire,"—flies by computer—while the pilot takes
a scheduled nap in the 17th hour of the 2-day flight,
5 minutes before the midair refueling of the clean burning engine

time for one short dream
in which your mother opens the screen door.

The facty heart, indiscernible
in graphite that absorbs trap-signals.
How will she find you?

Goddess of Mercy: I thought I saw Wife jump from this cliff

Wife: I jumped

Goddess of Mercy: I thought I saw Wife jump from this cliff
                          but the Valley is clean

Industrial Diamonds

Polycrystalline diamond-windows retaining transparence over wide-spectral regions never fog. Useless to write a backward message on. Notice how I pant at the clear window and yet my secret name never appears. It was never written. A diamond lens approaching atmospheric fires of Venus does not melt but burns completely without leaving ash, no Firebird singularly living again in its dusty body. Who is calling me from an additional line inside this house? No way of checking sleeping children without passing an eternity of rooms with open doors containing anonymous darknesses through which You walk prismy into the hall. In *Dreams*, a movie I'm remembering wrong, soldiers follow their Captain home from a battle. "Go back," he tells them, "Go back," so they march obediently back through the tunnel. I think theirs must have been so slow a death they never noticed it walking with them almost all the way back to the Capital. Diamond diamond-cutting blade with which diamond is sharpened.

"Jade Cabinet and One Last Thing," Anonymous

HANGING SCROLL
H: 167 CM. W: 85 CM.
MING (15TH C.?)

This is this life. Dawn Gate; the gate is locked. There is the gold of the gold pin
in Jade Cabinet's hair and the gold of Gold River. The bridge is wet; the gate is locked;
Dawn Gate good morning in which two gold anhingas dry gold wings perched upon pins
in Jade Cabinet's hair. Water bird inadequately evolved to swim and fly both in the same
hunt, no oil on the wings. Court Goldsmith says *for your daughter* to Jade Cabinet's
father.

The gold moon is the sun, it's that early. A night-guard hovers, perspective is such.
Or is that the afterlife? A life along side this life unintelligibly played in low lighting.
This is this life. A crowd in the foreground gathers in the dark. A crowd to the left
disperses. So these are clouds? Smoke from a faraway fire? Heaven's Honor Guard
forms on the furthest peak of the mountain. No. Flowers in uniform blue. Perspective
is such.

Much closer on a low hill the essence each figure exudes is dust off paper.
Centuries of unrolling have lent an uncertain glow to the painting.
Hesitance is a shade of gold in which Jade Cabinet can't see the night guard.
This is this life listening for one footstep in the world, one brow cocked to show
she hears one.

A Sculpture in the Garden

The complication that set this down
like a folded note on the breakfast table
prefers you read it in private;
but the subtle creases accentuated
in iron too cold to open
takes the light of traffic
into the vicinity of its metal folds. It just landed
and we can not call it ours, this origami-fortune
from another world
abbreviating something longer-winded
than what was said this morning.
It is the more important part of an argument
abstracted into form.
In another context
it was specific.
Here it sits on the lawn
as mere intention
to be alone.
If its confident sheen
turns you back at you
reflected in the strange accuracy
of its total dismissal of you,
you have understood.

At Shedd Aquarium

Watch them be themselves
in habitats contrived
in dark rooms with openings
like televisions broadcasting
a dimension where Pigment rides
in its original body
and metaphor initiates impractical
negotiations with Size and Color
and Speed and Silence
too thoroughly forward
but to feel
the self an excess.

Fastness, I am tired of resting.
Isn't it indecisive not to be smaller
driven through waters barely perceivable
but where a wake scribbles
a line like a Chinese character
abandoning its construction box
to slip as line only
into an opening
smaller than its shoulders?

Each fin scores the air
as it opens the surface.
A sliver of a fish circles
forever that day
as if to turn something over
in its skinny head keen
to resolve a difficulty
I have.

It is an opera with a lonesome
heroine pacing revolving moors
engineered to seem panoramic.
The diva opens and closes
the tragic mouth singing
deliberate, even breaths
intuition hears.

Theater of false proportion. Theater of constellations reconfiguring. Theater of
readjusting the reception. Theater of missing appointments. Theater of driving into
the ocean with the headlights turned lowest green and the theater of the engine
shifting into oceanic-overdrive. Theater of hearing something coming closer over
theatrical fields of theater set crops. Theater of this can not be my life, for which, it
is too quiet. Theater of seeing something moving in the one light in the distance
which is darkness. Theater of stopping. Theater of my mistake: not coming forward,
going further, the something moving in the theater of lighting in the theater of the
hour between the theater of morning and the theater of night in the theater of years
in which the theater of regret is keeping the secret theater of the revision.

Theater of slipping between
two points in a simulated rock-mountain.

Theater of who will not tell
casually follows.

Gypsy Rose

Losing one thing after another, Gypsy Rose
disappears as the scene changes.
Reveling in his disappointment,
the theater critic told her
I have a glove you threw to the audience
and hold it dear to me.
I have a strand of hair that was on that glove
the color of this hair here (he touched her then)
and asked her for her other glove.

Gypsy Rose removed the other glove
from her evening purse. First, she said,
shall I drop it beside me and you pretend
to have found it, and quite to my surprise, return
it and we shall fall in love forever after?
They rehearsed the scene and then performed it.

He said think of something that hurt you once, even if it was me,
and use that energy to drive the scene. It will be the impetus.
I have lost many things and the glove was one of them, she said to herself.

Does this belong to you, young lady?
Why yes it does. How kind of you to return it.
You have restored my hope
and I shall not begrudge one small kiss in return,
not on the lips, but here, where my glove would be.

Morikami Museum Garden

A game of opposites: losing a shoe into the carp pond in the garden
has a pond-equivalent of miraculously being given just one shoe.

Assume a shoe was already lost; the player is met by her reflection presenting
the replacement which both fits and suits; no cost to the player.

Is the shoe wet? It seemed it would be as it came toward the player out of the pond.
It was breaking the surface as it lifted heel-first over the rocks.
The player continues backward in considered steps over crab grass. Be grateful to
have both shoes on and step across the wooden bridge as if being rewound in a movie
silently past the scenery, approaching the beginning where a Japanese Lady prunes a
bonsai maple.

It must be a film about loss; you come from the middle of the reel in which you know
the bonsai gardener is a minor character—a prop of the first slow shot's meditative
detail. You long to hear the sharp shears open over an excessive brush of maple and
pare it down.
The lush opening of metal.
The clean mastery of the spare over the simple.
To just sit beside her in the marginal eye of the panning camera,
a drawn bird in the flourish of a scribe's wet pen bearing down on a first letter of a
first line of something long and beautiful and you are gold and inconsequential,
literally blown into place by the gold leafer.

The whole time you rewind over the wooden bridge you think about her. You are
backing up over a yellow hill.

In a demonstration on the lawn someone teaches children how to unfold origami
roses so that each crease is gone when the colored paper opens.

*

In a scene before a party you pull bobby pins from your hair and hold them in your lips: now you are ready to go. You come in with a man you don't know and are gradually let go by his hand. He takes the drink you're holding, stops talking and lets you go finally with his eyes.

Do you watch him back from the room? No. He will always be in the room once you go. You see him as you back through the door. Already it has no meaning. You back down a flight of stairs. It is a rare moment of abandon when you let the bottom of your skirt fall where it might get stepped on or trip you as you make your way down into the hall through two doors into the rain coming up from you, out of your hair and eyes, up off of your clothes, into the sky.

All to get back to the bonsai? Later you take everything back to the store. You give the cashier milk and a sandwich. He gives you money for them. Back into the road with nothing, months pass. It's the same road and store, and you have emptied your apartment. There's no food now and the light over the sink has come back on. That's nice, you think, when you wash your hands.

Rewinding further on, a different city. The reel is dark for hours.

*

This is the first time you are ever alone in rewind together
with a man you have loved until the beginning
of the film.
      He turns the light on to dress you
starting with the lowest of the buttons on your shirt.
He pushes each so slowly into its sliver as if he were threading a needle.
The scene again in delayed accuracy: the sun rising up your body,
button and button closing up the shirt.
Moment and moment closing in on the memory of it.
The zipper of the skirt rewinds up the hip
in the quickest distance

between points of undress.
How to describe anxiety temporally?
A slow, molten flower blooming casually where the first ribs meet.
In reverse, the flower closing. There is very little difference
between anticipation and regret. They meet in the same bed.

Women Contemplating Floating Fans (detail), 1625?

TWO PANELS FROM A THREE-PANEL FOLDING SCREEN

In Tahiti natives traded sex for the nails of the explorers' ship. Irresistible, cold utilitarian worked with the hammer's back from the hull where it was forced in and held its man just so. There's the *hold* of a ship but there is no *have*. In *Sparrows* Little Mary led orphans in silence through the bayou. No one follows you, little bell. Rigor mortis left you receiver in hand, a still in which Doctor Greenson is about to tell you there's no "motion" in "motion picture," no real "flow of action"— and while you ticked through the longest length of filmed walk elsewhere glasses were lifted to see the rabbit in the garden and the rabbit was lost.

Nails which had endured salts more tremulous than this were attached to necklaces cut from twine also used on the ship to hold something to something, like the two legs of the same dead pig. What disparate angel is this? There is a box that keeps opening. In *Niagara* there is a ship called "Maiden of the Mist" bringing tourists to the precipice. Every fall has a tour ship. A guide disembarks gently and stowaways rise like weevils in flour. O forthright Maiden, your diffuse body comes forward shivering to distinction, every inch of you sings to the President with the sequined suspension of a bridge. Distracted stage lights lap at the opera glasses of secret service agents and courtesans on the dusty bridge (it was gold leafed) cross businessmen to the missing edge.

Imagination

At Sarah's wedding when the groomsmen hoisted Sarah in a chair above our heads
she slid so gracefully off, each satin-covered button skimmed the seat. Tiny buttons,
there must have been two dozen up the bodice, each counted in a satin-covered ping
against the dinner chair. She hadn't eaten. Nerves and to close the dress.
The wisp of her loosened and came forward like love in a dream lewdly lights
a strange acquaintance whom it has possessed and made seductive.
Lofty thought, into the other imagination, lies down.
And not in dream only; light also resuggests objects on a real life table:
someone comes to breakfast and is no longer beautiful.
It must be the wind that keeps closing the closed door.
I keep thinking someone is coming up the back stairs when I remember
"back stairs" is a romantic construct of a different house in which servants no longer
even hurry about discreet quarters hidden beyond the bookcase.
It would be a good night

if each jolt was justified. It would mean so much
to wake up and know just what is needed. Listening to my neighbor practicing guitar
too slowly for the melody to grow familiar, I am with him, but he is alone.

Chantilly Lace

In wind so fierce flies breeding
themselves wingless by favoring the short-
winged over the soaring
of the species step one
step every hundredth year with
thread legs across the thread of being and being-
not, called by parish priests
"the devil's spit"—stitching in
air—this lace is a weather—blizzard of
figures upon the drape
hunting in a fog in
which dogs flow like a mist toward
the fox, same thread giving the fox pause, giving dogs chase,
threading them down a hole
beneath Château Chantilly
with the same coat of arms above,
below holding the leash.
One crow saw the icy opening in the ice.
Seldom left the fence.
But left the fence.
Not just light but breath
flows through the open work once called
"bone lace" for fishbone needles
recounting their needlework a vague
look to life as if seen
from under ice.
In Antarctica spiders whose webs
were so often blown
they bred themselves not to
need to spin them wake from
ice to find flies don't even fly.
Their lives are a long cold night
they wake from briefly

to feed for the afterlife. What
struggle to stay; what struggle to
escape. Pushing the lace curtain back,
arisen dead, cursed with the burden
to undo, are distracted from straying
by unworking the curtain itself.
With each stitch taken
a fox slips beneath.
But the pack unravels into
the foxhole too, and the forest fraying leaf by
leaf fills the pasture of
afterlife with oaks and threads
the bow of an assassin behind each.

House of De Beers

Sir Walter Raleigh etched a verse in a window glass
to Queen Elizabeth with his diamond ring, murky and listless,

table-facetted barely evenly enough to place a water glass, he pressed
the diamond into the pane with the glory of its chrysalis

100 miles under, surfaced in a rush underground Vesuvius
where there is no terror on no faces of no one devastated

and held in freeze-frame ash preserving
no one bending softly in a drawing

over the bed of someone who bought her.
There was a time when diamond was not prized in itself,

but as a tool to incise glass vases which were.
A peony opens. There is no wind in the heart

of the man who etched it.
In outline, the peony petals are clear

against the clarity of the vase.
Bend down and look through the empty centerpiece;

the other side of the room is unchanged
but everything is a specimen

of itself in a terrarium grown by a glassmaker
in which fire was blown breakable

and a glass overlay like
a layer of lace seemingly placed

as a measure of preservation
makes the soul more fragile.

YEAR 1867

In the pit-mines of South Africa,
stepped like the theater at Ephesus

miners rise with buckets of kimberlite tied to their belts
with their hands free above their heads

to show they have not got a raw diamond in either fist.
Underwhelming like sea glass, its glisten washed

in the tide of middle earth in which what's buried
comes back sitting up in its sleep

into this, our shared light, brushed by a feather brush.
How dreamy the diamond is before the face

is cut. Eurasamus Jacobs, searching for a stick
to unclog a drain stopped with the hair

of his sister, found one,
foggy like the moon of a moon.

The Colonial Secretary of Capetown
named it Eureka for what Archimedes said

discovering how to determine how much
of the King's

gold crown
is gold.

Entered in the Paris Exposition, 1867,
Austrian Empress

Elizabeth did not see it.
Too sick to make the trip

herself, a stamped
leather casket of

small exhibition
pictures was given to her.

She was so tired seeing this one —
a wall of milky clocks

behind a quiet row
of cane-back chairs —

that heaven must be like it,
chairs set out for everyone

although it would be too noisy
if we all are saved.

Carbon under pressure becomes both graphite
to mark an x on the sheep in the field

and diamond to write of my love in the window
which opens and closes as the thief goes in and out and in

(if this an inside job).
(It's not.)

Enough graphite was brought by armed coach from Keswick
with which to draw the whole route it took on 1 to 1 scale to London:

one mile of country road = one mile of depiction;
if it rains the armed guard pictured blends so with the wood behind him

I scarcely know him anymore. Not so with diamond:
it engraves with the precision of yes or no

when the question put is Did you recognize
the voice? Did you listen for the foot

on the stairs? Malleable, graphite accepts the shape put to it
and was used as a cannonball mold to mold imperfect cannonballs.

Imprecisely set down in field on fire, the siege of its diameter teems
like the concentric ripples of a stone in water.

YEAR 1862

Adam Worth rose from the list
of those dead at the second

Battle of Bull Run
and reenlisted across the line

a "Bounty Jumper," forthwith
dying differently for the South,

pushing the stone
back from the mouth of the cavern

(the son of a tailor) from whole cloth
stepping—a

Southern farmer now—
into the fray.

Luckily these
had no uniform

so he could slip back threadbare
into the Union Army

another bounty under his belt
(if he had one).

YEAR 1877

From his window at Kimberley Hotel
Adam Worth watched the miners searched outside

the makeshift Headquarters, one in a series built again
at the pit's edge, an edge encircling itself like lines

drawn around a bell to show it ringing in a drawing.
The pit-mine's edge advances through the rings

as if this pictured bell, drawn to show that those
across the ocean hear a ringing faintly, always for them

is loud enough to lead lost daughters
to their fathers' arms.

Adam Worth can see the miners pour the day's dirt
into a common vat, bend down, open mouths, and let

the guards' fingers under the tongue where miners have smuggled
a fortune in raw diamonds smooth as a button

feeding them to their horses and riding over the border
in silence until the horse is shot

and spliced with the expert knife of a cutpurse
digging now into the gut, breathless. Miners have cut their own thigh open

and sewn a diamond in. Lie down on me,
can you feel the diamond cutting the bone as I breathe?

The diamond in the hem of the dress
the tailor's wife had on when they came

breaking the glass for her went to the grave
shot with a pin still in her mouth

no doubt the diamond by now
is free.

YEAR 1878

Highway robbery was Adam Worth's first thought.
Does the vigilance of the Headquarters

relax in transport? He watched
guards load a bag (so small!) on the lap of the messenger

sitting in the stagecoach that turns down the path that turns
black everyday a few minutes

earlier. By the second week
it was dark long before the coach

reached the dock where they loaded one little pouch—
velvet in the imagination

hanging off the merchant's belt in paintings—
a cheap sackcloth sack, in fact,

like the bag slung over the feed clerk's fence
and loaded on the same ship bound

for England by way of India (who wants diamonds from
South Africa?) where among merchant seamen hoisting

bags of rice in the hold someone moves with a bag
as light as carob, for which the carat,

the primary unit, was named.
Adam Worth tied trip wire to opposite posts

across from one another at the point in the road
where it seemed to him that the driver and messenger

were already having the conversation they have here
where the air fills with the mating calls of insects like

an initial crackle of fat in a pan
distracting the horse, faster, now, where the road

runs downhill toward the water.
Since this is the year in California

a glass-plate series of stills was taken of a horse
in each of its postures

to prove for money that it hovers momentarily
above the earth

I'll tell you
both sets of the horse's legs lift in one frame of thought,

the front legs lift as the neck rears
meeting the back a moment after

kicking the shadow to rise
over speculation

into debt.
Adam Worth

ran into the woods
without the diamonds

when the stagecoach driver
cocked his rifle.

Another thing I'll tell you: when the conjurer of images
Georges Méliès paused to fix his camera

while a horse cab emerged from a tunnel,
it ran again

just as a hearse replaced the cab,
seeming when projected

that God had spoken
of the life span of the passenger

whose little hand was not visible inside
fanning and fanning herself

in fever. But this is years from now;
why should I tell you

how pleased he was
with the edit?

YEAR 1879

I cultivated the trust of the postman who held the key for months,
a year passed and we were meeting in the city's one teashop.

Posing as a dealer of hat feathers I opened shop not far from the post office
where the diamonds are kept locked in a wall of boxes like a dovecote.

In dream the glottal cooing an aviary this size would make came to me,
but truly it was silent there but for a telegram being pecked out occasionally

from far away so quietly I half envied the postman and told him so, hearing only
the one bird of transmission instead of the sound rising like a cloud

above the boys I hired to chase them down in a cage, I told him, was on the farm
where my wife is and I believed me and began to love you.

I finally told the postman after months of knowing him that my neck was on the line over a
shipment. Although the post office was closed and his clerk long gone could he get it

for me himself? Alone at the counter I took the key from the hook.
Pressed it into a wax copy and returned it.

I'm sorry, I told the postman, thanked him,
sorry to trouble you, and left sorry-looking with the postman

even stopping with him, key-relief burning in my pocket, for tea; package I was sorry
to bother about, on the empty seat beside me. Oh sorry night

isn't it sad to think about me sending this box to myself. It passed for feathers, it was
empty.

Because I paid a child to pay a child to cut the mast tomorrow
the ship that comes each evening to take the diamonds won't be coming.

Instead, they'll be locked up in their pigeon hole where the key I cut
from a tin cup with the wax impression I took

will lead me down the same path its sister walks in good faith.
This is to say that when you get this, why not start out to meet me.

You might bring the opera glasses to make me out among those coming by horse—
two on each, one dying and one dying in his arms.

You'll know me by my approach.
I'm coming on foot with a diamond in my mouth.

Notes

The final passages of "House of Worth" adapt lines written by Martin Gale on Sarah Bernhardt, April 15, 1899. I encountered the passage in Robert Horville's, "The Stage Techniques of Sarah Bernhardt," printed in Eric Salmon's (ed. and trans.) *Bernhardt and the Theatre of Her Time* (Connecticut: Greenwood Press, 1984).

The lines regarding the natural history of platinum in "House of Cartier" are gleaned from the words of Mary Elvira Weeks in *Discovery of the Elements* (Pennsylvania: Mack Printing Co., 1933).

The italicized passages in "Tiffany & Co." are tailored with sentences in Marta Braun's *Picturing Time: The Work of Etinee-Jules Maray (1830–1904)* (Illinois: University of Chicago Press, 1992) and Vachel Lindsay's 1915 essay "Thirty Differences between the Photoplays and the Stage," reprinted in *Awake in the Dark: An Anthology of American Film Criticism, 1915 to the Present*, edited by David Denby (New York: Vintage Books, 1977). The lines belonging to Leo Tolstoy's *Anna Karenina* are adapted from the English translation by Louise and Aylmer Maude.

Coco Chanel's remark in "Chanel N° 5 " is quoted in Janet Wallach's biography of her, *Chanel* (New York: Doubleday, 1998).

"House of Versace" leans on the account of the death of Helen Jewett told by Patricia Cline Cohen in *The Murder of Helen Jewett: The Life and Death of a Prostitute in Nineteenth-Century New York* (New York: Vintage Books, 1999). She writes, "[I]f the suspect touched the corpse, and the corpse bled fresh blood, it was taken as a powerful sign of guilt in seventeenth-century New England. The all-seeing eye of God provided such signs to leave no doubt as to guilt." Throughout the poem, some of the testimony is invented and some echoes Cohen quoting the Coroner's Inquest, April 10, 1836, *People vs. Robinson*, District Attorney's Indictment Papers and the official testimonies of witnesses at the trial. In regard to the issue of the mended cloak, Cohen observes "It took a woman's eye, a woman's knowledge of sewing, to identify the one idiosyncratic feature that made it Robinson's cloak and his alone." My rendering of this detail is entwined with Ariadne's description of leading Theseus from the labyrinth in Ovid's *Heroides*. As for the murder weapon, Cohen writes, "Some 2,500 such hatchets were produced in 1834, the owner of the New York firm that stamped its name on the handles testified at the trial, and they were sold all over the city. The porter in Hoxie's store used such a hatchet to open boxes and crates. James Wells said he had last seen the store's hatchet on the Wednesday before the murder, but he did not miss it until the following Monday morning. . . ."

"Devil Finch" nearly quotes the line from the *Song of Songs*, "Draw me after you, let us make haste./ The king has brought me into his chambers." In Edgar Allan Poe's "The Tell-Tale Heart," the narrator "heard all things in the heaven and in the earth."

The quoted passage concluding "Vampire Finch" is adapted from the words of Moshe and Elie Garbarz in *A Survivor*, translated by Jean-Jacques Garbarz (Michigan: Wayne State University Press, 1992).

I learned about Adam Worth's diamond theft in South Africa in Ben MacIntyre's *The Napoleon of Crime: The Life and Times of Adam Worth, Master Thief* (New York: Farrar, Straus and Giroux, 1997).

Kuhl House Poets

Bin Ramke *Airs, Waters, Places*

Robyn Schiff *Worth*

Cole Swensen *Such Rich Hour*

Emily Wilson *The Keep*